SPIRITUAL
IMPLANTS

POCKET EDITION

Published from
Mardukite Borsippa HQ, San Luis Valley, Colorado
Mardukite Academy & Systemology Society
for spiritual or educational purposes only

SPIRITUAL IMPLANTS

Systemology
Professional Course
Booklet #11

Developed by Joshua Free
for the Systemology Society

© 2023, JOSHUA FREE

ISBN : 978-1-961509-36-8

Pocket Paperback Edition — *December 2023*

mardukite.com

Chart Your Flight For Ascension...
Then Let Your Spirit Fly!

Unlock your ultimate spiritual potential by removing barriers to your true native state.

Learn how to easily attain Self-actualization and help to actualize others along the way.

A greater appreciation and understanding of *Spiritual Life* and *Existence* awaits you. Expand your reach to achieve your dreams.

Each 'Professional Course' lesson-booklet offers simple exercises and techniques that directly apply the philosophy of Systemology, assisting to increase your true knowingness, improve your capabilities in this life, and even decide what you will do in your next.

At the Mardukite Academy of Systemology, the 'Professional Course' lessons in this series are presented to Seeker's that have already completed the 'Basic Course', previously released as six lesson-booklets, or the six-in-one single volume edition "Fundamentals of Systemology."

This all new presentation of the Systemology 'Pathway-to-Ascension' takes Seekers and continuing students from "Zero" to "Infinity" at lightning-fast speeds!

Discover Who You Really Are...
Because You Were Never Human

...more titles in this series coming soon!

TABLET OF CONTENTS

COURSE INTRODUCTION

LESSON ELEVEN:
SPIRITUAL IMPLANTS

APPENDIX

PROFESSIONAL
COURSE
INTRODUCTION

WELCOME, SEEKER!
LET'S CHART YOUR JOURNEY
ON THE PATHWAY

Systemology is a "holistic" approach to understanding the human experience. It is not actually a singular "subject" in itself, but rather, a new way in which to view the many subjects of *Life* and all *Existence.*

This is a professional course in *Systemology*—specifically, how to *apply* the spiritual philosophy of *Mardukite Systemology* as a personal *"Pathway"* to Ascension. Our *Systemology* is a new approach to *"Self-Actualization."* It is completely relevant for the modern age and the future; and quite different from any previous similar attempts, or other traditions, you might find. What's more: it is applicable to anyone with any background.

This *"Professional Course"* series of lessons (booklets) immediately follows the material given in the *"Basic Course"* series—available as six separate pocket-sized booklets, or in a single hardcover volume titled: *"Fundamentals of Systemology: A New Thought For The 21st Century."*

This is a *new* presentation of *Systemology*, emphasizing the application of our philosophy for those *Seekers* that are *"Flying-Solo"*—or else working through their studies and exercises as solitary practitioners. This is a new innovation for *Systemology*. Aside from the book *"Crystal Clear,"* all of our former advanced courses have placed a focus on *"Traditional Piloting"*—where experienced practitioners assist *Seekers* in *"processing."*

To receive the greatest benefit from this study: it is expected that a *Seeker* will already be familiar with the fundamental concepts and terminology (previously relayed in the *Basic Course*) before using lessons from the *Professional Course*. This will allow us to cover the extensive territory of the *Pathway* much more quickly. However, for reference, a basic *"glossary"* of vocabulary used in this lesson is provided in the *"appendix."*

A NEW VIEW OF THE HUMAN SPIRIT

Systemology is not a religion and does not require any type of *faith*. It is, however, built upon a "spiritual" premise—and as such is an "applied spiritual philosophy." It is based on ancient teachings that we are *Spiritual Beings* essentially "wearing" bodies like clothes—or using them as "vehicles." Yet our true native nature is not *physical*, but beyond this existence; and we can certainly operate a "body" from *outside* of it.

13

We are **all** *Spiritual Beings*—each of us a *unit* of *Spiritual Awareness*—that have experienced a very long *Spiritual Timeline* of existence. Although we might be particularly attached to the familiar "physical shells" associated with *this* lifetime, our true *"Spiritual Lifetime"* is seemingly *eternal*. We have been many things before *Human*, and we go onward as a *Spiritual Being* after our *"genetic vehicle"* of *this* incarnation perishes.

While a "spiritual" view of the *Human Condition* may not seem unique to our philosophy, just how often is the concept treated *systematically*? For that matter: just how many people, supposedly raised to this or that religion, or professing to believe one thing or another, actually live their lives as though they are *Spirits?*

As *Spiritual Beings* of immortal existence and infinite potential, we are not simply the *"creations"* of an even greater *Being-*

ness; we are, in fact, an integral part of that *"creative force"* which permeates all existence.

Our basic nature is to be a *"creative being"*—our highest goals are *"to create."* And as such a being—which we refer to as an *Alpha-Spirit* in *Systemology*—we have run into some difficulties along the course of our *Spiritual Timeline* and found ourselves trapped within material *Universes* of our own collaborative *creation*.

Since we did not start out our existence in a trapped condition, it is correct to say that we have *"fallen"* from our native *"godlike"* states. It did not happen all at one, but progressively and systematically. We know our "troubles" have resulted from accumulated "barriers" and "blockages"—or *fragmentation*—during our vast experiences as *Spiritual Beings*. They are not because we lack something; but because of what's been added.

In *Systemology*, we systematically examine those routes by which we must have descended to reach our present condition, then reverse the direction of travel and chart a personal *"Pathway to Ascension."* Of course, the exact "details" of the *Spiritual Timeline* will be different for each individual *Seeker*. However, we have been able to systematically chart our *Pathway* based on common patterns of *Human fragmentation*.

In the most basic terms: the *fragmentation* that defines our "downward spiral" consists of decisions or considerations where we deny our true nature. This includes those decisions to *"withdraw"* rather than *"reach"*; where we choose to *not-know* rather than *know*; to *not-communicate* rather than *communicate*; and ultimately, to take *no-responsibility* for being a *creative-cause*, and therefore succumb to being an *effect*.

16

But there is *hope!* And much more importantly: there is an effectively workable *way out* of the mazes and traps of our existence. If you are reading this now, you have already begun to gather your tools and build up the *"horsepower"* necessary to break the gravity holding your *Spiritual Beingness* to the *Human Condition.*

STUDYING THE
PROFESSIONAL COURSE

Most *Seekers* study and practice *Systemology* at-a-distance and independent of the "Mardukite Academy" or any "Master-level" mentors trained therein. This means that the *books* (and to a lesser degree, the *internet*) are the only means of direct contact a *Seeker* maintains with the "Systemology Society" during their studies. A continuing *Seeker* from the *"Basic Course"* will be familiar with the style of study found in *this* course.

Misunderstood words are the most common reason an individual abandons studying a subject. When a misunderstanding occurs, *Awareness* declines. These misunderstandings start to "stack up" after the first occurrence, and as a result, the level of interest and attention will also decline. This is how a "confusion" develops; and the individual will get "bored" with the subject, feel tired, and unable to concentrate.

One solution is to return to the part of the material that was still interesting and enjoyable to read. When scanning around that area of text, there is likely to be a new word (or new specific use of a familiar word) that is unclear, but was passed by unnoticed. All *Systemology* books include their own *glossary*. Using this *glossary* and a high-quality dictionary will help resolve this misunderstanding once it is located.

An effective education of any subject is taught on a *gradient*. This is what is intended by presenting the study of something as "*grades*." Rather than treating a subject as one total mass, true learning is achieved by increasing one's understanding with a *gradual* increase upward. The *ascent* to a mountaintop is not successfully achieved in one leap, but by targeting and reaching specific checkpoints along the way.

This *Professional Course* consists of a series of lessons (booklets) that gradually increase a *Seeker's* ability to understand and apply the practices and techniques of *Systemology* as a complete "*Pathway to Ascension*." It is an appropriate study for continuing *Seekers* (from the *Basic Course*), but also "advanced" *Systemologists*.

Each lesson (booklet) of the *Professional Course* applies *Systemology* to a particular subject (or focus). It is best if the entire course can be studied and applied in sequential order. These lessons also employ a style of practice or technique called *"Systematic Processing."* An introduction to applying this methodology is provided in the final lesson (booklet) of the *Basic Course*—or in the *"Fundamentals of Systemology"* volume.

To study the *Professional Course* just like a student at the Academy: a *Seeker* reads through all instructional material and applies each exercise (or *"process"*) presented in the text to the extent they comfortably can, before continuing on to the next lesson (booklet).

When first starting on the *Pathway* as a *Solo* practitioner, without the aid of an experienced *Pilot*, a *Seeker* shouldn't "push too hard" or allow themselves to get too "stuck" on any one area (lesson) or *process*. It is not expected that any one area will be completely handled when first introduced. For optimum results, it is expected that a serious *Seeker* will make more than one "pass" through the entire *Professional Course.*

The *Professional Course* is not altogether different from other forms of practical or technical education: where the instruction and exercises are delivered to a completion, and then a student further increases their abilities, strength and skill-level by applying additional practice throughout their life. Therefore, a student should not concern themselves with perfectly mastering each step (or lesson) before progressing forward.

Additional passes through the material are likely to result in different "*realizations*" (an increased *level of understanding*) than a previous time. New "layers" of *Knowingness* may now be accessible during a *process* that may not have been before. It is important to avoid invalidating the progress you've made just because one area is not completely handled right away, or if a certain *process* seems too difficult on the first pass.

CHARTING A COURSE ON THE PATHWAY

Although we can communicate a systematic structure to *fragmentation,* the personal journey experienced along the *Pathway* will be different for each *Seeker.* For example, certain areas will seem more *"turbulent"* or difficult for one *Seeker* than another. We tend to say that these areas have more *"charge"* on them—or that they are more *"heavily charged."* It is best to handle such areas when you are already feeling "good" and not in a situation (or condition) where that specific area is consistently being *"triggered"* or *"restimulated."*

As an applied philosophy, *Systemology* "theory" can be easily utilized in the "laboratory" of the "world-at-large" in everyday life. This is implied within the basic instruction of each lesson. Unlike other "sciences" that conduct experiments by making a change to some "objective variable" *out there* and waiting to see an effect, our focus is the individual (or *Observer*) themselves, and how *they* affect the "*Reality*" perceived.

In addition to applying *Systemology* "New Thought" to everyday life, our philosophy is applied by using specific exercises and systematic techniques. These "*processes*" provide the most stable personal gain (and *realizations*) for each area; but only when actually applied with a *Seeker's* full "*presence*" and *Awareness*.

This *Professional Course* is designed so that it may be easily read and studied with little concern for what "dangers" these teachings—or *processing*—might unleash. However, there are still some guidelines that pertain to the "best-uses" of these course lessons, particularly if a *Seeker* intends for stable development.

Skipping over too much material/*processing* in early lessons may make attempts to understand (or apply) later lessons more difficult. However, once the complete *Professional Course* is worked through at least once in its entirety, specific areas can then be later returned to and treated with a greater sense of *Awareness* and *"presence"* than before. Of course, in *"Traditional Piloting,"* the rate of processing is monitored by an experienced practitioner; but in *"Solo-Processing,"* a *Seeker* must regulate their own progress on the *Pathway*.

Applying a systematic technique is called *"running a process."* The *processes* are designed with very simple instructions or "*command-lines*." To *run* a *processing command-line*, a *Seeker* may be assisted by the communication of that *line* from a "*Co-Pilot*" (as in "*Traditional Piloting*"). But even then, a *Seeker* must still personally "input" the *command* as *Self*. For this reason —and quite thankfully— *Solo-Processing* is possible.

TAKING FLIGHT ON THE PATHWAY

Processing Techniques are intended to treat the *Spiritual Being* or *Alpha-Spirit*; the individual themselves. It is applied by the *Alpha-Spirit*—then *Self-directed* to the "Mind-System" or even a "body" (*genetic-vehicle*), both of which are "constructs" that the *Alpha-Spirit* (*Self*, or the "I-AM" *Awareness* unit) operates, but neither of which is actually *Self*. *Fragmentation* causes *Humans* to falsely identify *Self as* the "*Mind*" or even a "*Body*."

The *Professional Course* lessons (booklets) are designed for the *Beginning Seeker* in mind—one that may have an understanding of theory, but with little experience in practice. That being said: each of these lessons may be used toward total *Beta-Defragmentation* within a specific area. There are also more *processes* given for each subject than may be necessary to achieve an *ultimate end-point realization* on that entire area.

Some *processes* can be treated quite lightly at first; others may require a bit of working at in order to get *"running"* well. It is important to set aside a period of time when you can be dedicated to your studies and *processing*. This period of time is referred to as a *"processing session."* The reason for this, is that when a *process* does start *running* well, it is important to be able to complete it to a satisfactory *"end-point."*

The purpose of *systematic processing* is to be able to *really* "look" at things and even determine the *considerations* we have made—or attitudes we have decided—about *Reality* as a result of those experiences. It doesn't do us much good to simply "glance"—or to *restimulate* something uncomfortable and then quickly *withdraw* from it once again, leaving more of our *attention* yet again behind and held fixedly on it.

Generally speaking, a *Seeker* continues to *run* a *process* so long as something is "happening"—which is to say, the *process* is still producing a change. Usually this is evident by the type of "answers" that a *command-line* helps a *Seeker* originate from the database of their own *Mind-System*. The *command-lines* do not "do" anything on their own. They assist a *Seeker* to direct their own attention toward increasing *Awareness*.

Of course, a *Seeker* may also cease to generate new "data" from a *process* without reaching an *"ultimate" realization* as an *"end-point."* It is possible that additional "layers" (or even other "areas") require handling before anything "deeper" is accessible. If this is the case, end the *process.* But, if a *Seeker* is *withdrawing* from something uncomfortable that was incited or stirred up, then a *process* is *run* until they feel "good" about it.

In case the thought of encountering *"turbulence"* is a concern: the techniques given as *"Opening Procedures"* of a *Formal Session* (in the *Basic Course*), and those found in the earliest lessons of the *Professional Course,* are quite useful when applied as "safety nets" for maintaining *Awareness* and *presence,* even when *Flying-Solo.*

One of the benefits to *Flying-Solo* is that *processing* is entirely *Self-determined.* This

28

already provides a certain built-in "safety" for a practitioner. Anything you *restimulate* by *Self-determinism* is *your thing*. It is not incited by external *other-determined* influences (or other "source-points" in existence) that make you an *effect*. It can be more easily handled in *processing*—or you can simply let things "cool down" and come back to it again.

While it may seem "mysterious" to beginners, a *Seeker* gets a sense for knowing how long to *run* a *process* only with practice. Once you have spent some time actually applying the *Professional Course*, there are many aspects that become "second nature" because they are, in fact, a part of our true original nature. All we have done is *"reverse engineer"* the routes of *creation* and *consideration* that are already *our own*.

LESSON ELEVEN:
SPIRITUAL
IMPLANTS

BEYOND BETA-DEFRAGMENTATION

Depending on the extent to which a *Seeker* has *run* the former *processing-levels* —and, of course, the amount of *highly-charged past incidents* that have been *confronted* and *defragmented*—the first primary stable state of *"Beta-Defragmentation"* is often experienced by the end of our former lesson (booklet) for *Systemology Level-4* (in combination with all previous lessons).

Systemology Level-5 begins with this present *Professional Course* lesson (booklet); and this *processing-level* serves as an additional *"booster"* or *"stabilizer"* for basic *"Beta-Defragmentation"* –and– as a *"primer"* for *"upper-level"* work (as preparation for additional *Advanced Ability* training and *Alpha-Defragmentation*).

The benefit from this *level* only comes

after accomplishing the previous work on the *Pathway*. The material in *this* and *future* lessons does not replace the training, skill and increased *Awareness* that is gained *only* by properly following the *systematic procedure* outlined for *Systemology Level-0 to 4*.

Once sufficient training and skill in previous *processing-levels* is attained, a *Seeker* may even continue to use any of those techniques (as they best apply) to handling whatever comes up in *sessions* (and *Life*) thereafter. Increased *certainty* (and *willingness*) in being able to "handle" (or *confront*) "*Existence*" is what opens up more "data" from the "*Backtrack*" (or one's personal "*Spiritual Timeline*") for *processing*. [Much of the material given in this lesson is based on lecture transcripts (from *March 2023*) published as "*Systemology: Backtrack*" or "*Advanced Systemology: Academy Lectures, Volume 6.*"]

Too often it has been found that there is a

certain "glamour" or "excitement" attached to exploring the *Backtrack*—or the "uncovering" of *"past-life"* memory, *&tc.* But, often times, an individual does not realize the true reason that this information is hidden; they don't realize just how much *attention* (or in essence, *energy* or *effort*) has been placed on "blocking it out" (as a *Spiritual Being* with *that* ability).

Our methods promote getting a "handle on" what has taken—and *is* taking—place in *this* *"Lifetime"* before chasing down accumulated *fragmented imprints* from countless *"past-lives."* However, at a "higher level" of *realization*, we *recognize* that an individual or *Alpha-Spirit* has *one continuous "Spiritual Timeline"* that is merely being *experienced* as relatively separate *forms* or *bodies* (*"incarnations"*) and in various *Universes.*

In addition to *processing* exercises and techniques, the *upper-levels* of the *Professional Course* also begin to emphasize a more "expert" handling of *systematic processing* (*sessions*) in general. This not only allows a *Solo-Pilot* to handle more "advanced" material on their own, but also increases the *certainty* that a *Seeker* might have to *Pilot* another.

As the title of this course suggests, a *Seeker* completing it will have earned the minimum requirements to *professionally* or *vocationally* provide (*Pilot*) "Beta-Defragmentation" procedures (*Systemology Level-0 to 4*) for others—to assist the *Self-Actualization* and *Ascent* of other *Seekers*. While this is not the primary goal of this *Professional Course*, most *Seekers* find that "wanting to share it" is a natural side-effect of its completion.

"*Helping Others*" is actually one of the few activities—apart from *systematic processing*—that effectively takes the "weight" off the type of areas we *defragment* on the *Pathway to Ascension*. But, of course, before we can most effectively and clearly *help* others, we must first have *helped* ourselves reach a point of such personal stability that we can safely and appropriately extend our *reach downward* to lend a *helping hand*.

IDENTIFYING "SOURCES"

To handle the *Backtrack*, advanced concepts of *"Spiritual Implanting,"* or even to have a better understanding of *Life-experiences* in general, it is important to understand *who* is doing the *looking*. The more *"metaphysical"* techniques and exercises of previous *processing-levels* are intended to provide a *Seeker* with greater *certainty* on *"Self as the Alpha-Spirit"* (rather than *identifying Self* as a *"personality-package"* or any kind of *"body"*).

By this point along the *Pathway*, it is critical for a *Seeker* to focus directly on improving their *"Awareness as a Spiritual Being"* in order to "break free" from more "attachments" associated with artificial *"personalities"* and *"identifications."* This is what provides stability to a *Beta-Defragmented* state, which in turn allows for "higher-level" advancement in those "areas" that are now more available due to previous *processing*.

Anything that an *Alpha-Spirit* carries (*compulsively continuously*) along its own *"Spiritual Timeline"* is a product or *creation* of its own *considerations* and *Alpha-Thought/"postulates,"* however much these might also have been coerced, *enforced*, "implanted," or otherwise influenced, from outside *"other-determined" sources* along the way. A "high-power" *Awareness* that *this is* what's happening is *"Step-One"* to its *undoing*.

To reinforce this idea, we direct the first exercise of this *processing-level* toward *spotting sources*. By *"source,"* we mean

38

what is *"originating"* or *"causing"* something—for example, a "place" or "point" of origin, from which something comes (or is *communicated*). At this time, we are mainly interested in simply *running* through the *considerations* that occur in *processing* much more than whether or not we are "correct." This may be practiced with any "condition" or "situation" that interests the *Seeker* (or else, an area that is being *defragmented*).

A. *"Spot something that could be a 'source' for ---."*

B. *"Spot something that is probably not a 'source' for ---."*

By this point, a *Seeker* should be familiar with the use of *"spotting"* in a *processing command-line* ("PCL")—but, this time, we are not restricting our *"range of view"* to only that which is physically present in the room or environment. We mean to specifically direct *attention* and *Awareness* onto something—including, for example:

"*mental imagery*" or "*memory*" that is not, itself, a part of *Beta-Existence* (*reality* that others also can *view*), but are *actual* experiences (or even reflections of the *Back-track*) that the individual (*Alpha-Spirit*) "sees" (or *Knows*).

An inability to *identify* even a single *source* indicates a high degree of *fragmentation* (or low-*Awareness*). By this, we mean too, that they are unable to be "in communication" with their environment. Such individuals appear (to others) quite "out-of-touch" since they are obviously also misappropriating *cause* for *Reality* and *Existence*—and may also be still quite enamored by other "*mystical*" and "*magickal*" traditions or beliefs.

A *Seeker* that is unable to *identify anything* as a "*source*" or "*cause*" of *anything* is likewise unable *to be* a *Self-Determined* "*source*" or "*cause*" themselves (at least *knowingly*). Of course, people are *causing* things all the time; but their level of

Awareness determines just how *Self-Directed* those actions (or behaviors) truly are.

We began with a more direct *process* "about something" for practice—but a more *general process* for this area is:

A1. *"Spot a source."*

A2. *"Notice something about it."*

B1. *"Spot a non-source."*

B2. *"Notice something about it."*

There are some *Seekers* that quickly spot *"Self"* as the only *"source"* (as an *end-realization*) and then move off from the *process*. Not only does this miss the point of the *process*, it is also inaccurate. A *Seeker* that *only* identifies themselves as a *source*, will experience wide fluctuations between states of *"mania"* and *"guilt."* Of course, when high-power *Awareness* is applied to *perceiving sources* and *causes*, the effects of *fragmentation* easily fall away.

For additional practice, perform the following exercise in a public place. These "PCL" may be used fully on various different "*terminals*" in a single *process*, or you may alternate the ("*B*"-*Steps*) on a single *terminal*. Just continue *running* it (as it works best for you) until there is a *realization*, things seem "brighter," and/or you are "feeling good" about the *process*.

A. "*Spot a person (or lifeform).*"

B1. "*Notice something they are causing.*"

B2. "*Notice something they are not causing.*"

And finally, whether *processing* indoors or outdoors, select a small object or portion of wall to look at. Then *run* the following *considerations* alternately "on it" until there is a change in *Awareness*, or one of the *end-points* just described previously (above). Most of the upper-level *processes* are simply *run* until such points. Additionally, in this case, as you cycle through these PCL multiple times (and eventually using different objects, &tc.), focus on increasing the sense you have of *"Step-1"* each time you *run* the *process.*

1. *"Get the concept that you are creating it."*

2. *"Get the concept that others are creating it."*

3. *"Get the concept that no one is currently creating it."*

IDENTIFYING "WHAT-IS"

Even when only nearing the completion of an effectively *run Beta-Defragmentation* regimen, a *Seeker* should arrive at the *realization* that the *Alpha-Spirit*—the I-AM, the actual *Self*—is *"non-local"*; that its true *Beingness* is not *actually located* within the *"space-time"* of *this*, or any, *"Beta-Existence."*

While experiencing the *Human Condition,* an *Alpha-Spirit* has rigidly fixed its own *"point-of-view"* (POV) to a *singular view-*

43

point that *is* "*local.*" But, any *identification* related with "this *viewpoint*" as being the same as "one's own personal *Beingness*" is purely a matter of *associative considerations*; which makes it "*real*" (for purposes of experiencing a *reality*), but not "*actual.*"

In *actual fact*, the *Alpha-Spirit* has never really left from its original "*static*" position as a "*unit*" of *Spiritual Awareness* (that is *aware* of being *aware*). It has, however, manifested many "*postulates*" of *creation*, many "layers" of *consideration*, and of course, *reality-agreements* regarding our ability to be in "*communication*" with others in a "*Shared Universe.*" All of this contributes to what we call "*Existence.*"

The pattern of accumulating *fragmentation* and subsequent *condensation* or *solidification* of *Universes* (*Existence*) — as reflected on the *Backtrack* — suggests that we are experiencing cycles of a "downward spiral." Of course, this is not the "bedtime story" that we reveal to *Seekers*

44

early on the *Pathway*. It is not meant to be discouraging—but it does indicate how critical *defragmentation* is to the "*Spiritual Being.*" Because it will go on *existing eternally*, but only *experiences* what it considers *to exist*.

Just as a high-power *attention* on *actual* "*sources*" and "*causes*" will elevate a *Seeker's Actualized Awareness*, so too do we find an additional boost in stability and certainty when a *Seeker* becomes *more aware* of the *existence* of the *actual* in contrast to the *non-existence* of the *non-actual*. As with "*sources,*" this is important for high-level *defragmentation* of "*imprints*" and "*implants*" (stemming from further on the *Backtrack*).

In *Systemology*, when we talk about *reality*, and *control* over our experience of *existence*, we are actually talking about "*creation*" and "*what-Is*"—"*Is*" with a capital "*I*"—such as our handling of the "*IS-factors*" (discussed previously in *Systemo-*

logy Level-4). Very often, a *Seeker's* personal conception of *"what-Is"* will be greatly affected by *where* on the *Backtrack* (the *imprint* or *incident*) that much of their own *attention* "units" are *still* "stuck," "hung up" or "suspended" on (as *fragmentation*). The nature (or qualities) of such an *incident* (if not the *incident* itself) might even *resurface* by alternating the following PCL:

A. *"What is?"*
B. *"What isn't?"*

In *Traditional Piloting*, a *professional* uses such a *process* to monitor and increase the "present-time" *presence* that a *Seeker* is currently applying to higher-level *processes*. Is there *presence* really in the *past*? —having more *attention* stuck on past incidents; past *IS-ness* (such as with *"psychosis"*). Are they actually *present* in the *present*—or just continuously *"stuck"* in the *present*, as with *"neurotic"* tendencies?

The ultimate goal would be to get a *Seeker* to collect all their *attention-units* up and have them back under *Self-directed control*.

A *Seeker* should answer from a *present-time viewpoint* for several cycles of the *process* before moving off of it. What is more likely to happen, is that a *Seeker* will start with *present-time existences* and then move further *back* in the *past* before coming back to the *present-time existences*. It is also possible that a *Seeker* may start with distantly *past existences* first. In any case, the *process* ends when *only present existences* are coming up (or being consistently repeated).

For an additional (less "esoteric") *process*: *consider* the following, in alternation.

A. *"What must be a part of your existence?"*

B. *"What must not be a part of your existence?"*

If you were to add another *"circuit"* to this *process*, you would also *run* *"must/must not"* for *"another's"* existence. And finally, we apply an *objective process*, using a large object or wall—spending a few minutes holding the *concept* suggested by each of the following PCL as they are cycled.

A. *"Get the idea that it is there."*

B. *"Get the idea that it is not there."*

C. *"Maintain both ideas simultaneously."*

Having done all this, let's step out a bit further by applying this practice to another *objective process*—which also uses the walls of a room. Once seated comfortably, with eyes open, *look at the wall*, then *visualize* that it is "transparent" or "see-through" (which is to say *create* an "empty space" where the wall currently is). Now, *imagine looking through the wall* and seeing what is on the other side.

You can practice this with different walls

in the same room—then different rooms
—*spotting* things through the wall. Don't
be overly concerned with accuracy (or
checking to see if you are right); just work
with this as best you can until you "feel
good" about your practice.

"CONDITIONS" & "SIGNIFICANCES"

When we speak of a specific manner or
state of *Beingness, IS-factors*—and various
other things that either are essential for,
or modify, *existence*—we are referring to
"*conditions*." For example: *fragmentation*,
itself, is a *condition*. It restricts the nature
of things in one system and causes or allows things in another. Another example:
the experience of *Beta-Existence* (this *Universe*) is composed of many *conditions*. It
requires a specialized package of *fragmentation* in order to compulsively and
fixedly experience the *Human Condition*.

Properly *identifying conditions* and how they were handled (meaning, what we did about it, and/or what *considerations* we still maintain from it) is critical for *de-fragmenting* areas that are not targeted directly in former *processing-levels*. The reason for holding off on this until now, is that high-power *Awareness* is required.

Although it may not occur, it is very likely that a deep source of *turbulence* will *resurface*. If and when this happens, do not change *processes* just because an un-desirable experience is encountered. The *fragmentation* or *imprinting* must be *con-fronted* and *processed-out* by repeatedly us-ing this same *systematic process* (if it is this *process* that *resurfaced* it). If necessary, you can always "soften the impact" of *con-fronting* by noticing (or *spotting*) some-thing about what you are handling, and alternately *spotting* something in the room (*present*).

Many *conditions* and *considerations* may

have to be *run* in this *process* until the "target" *imprint* or *incident* is *identified*. It is possible that it does not *resurface* during the first *session* that this *process* is applied. The ultimate goal here is to *identify* the *single imprint* or *incident* (for an area) that the *Seeker* is still *persistently creating* or *carrying* into "*present-time.*" The concern for this type of *processing* is not how long it is *run* while still "missing the target," but whether it gets *overrun* beyond the purposes described in this section.

The *general process* is:

A. "*Spot an existing condition.*"
B. "*What have you done about that?*"

In *Traditional Piloting*, the first PCL is only repeated if a *Seeker* needs to refocus *attention* for answering the second. By this, we mean an individual is likely to have *done* many things about a *single condition*. When all of the *considerations* for a *condition* are *processed*, you can then *run* it on another *condition* within the same *session*. If *identifying* and *spotting* (in the *process*) are not sufficient in directing high-power *Awareness* toward *defragmentation*, then a more direct PCL may be added to the second part, such as: *"What part of that can you confront?"*

Although a *Seeker* is able to remember (or *recall*) many different past *incidents*—and while there would seem to be many *imprints* that require *defragmentation*—there is likely to be *one* truly significant *imprinting incident* that has been persistently carried forth into the present, upon which all other *imprinting* is "stacked up" on. This originating *incident* would then act as a *"platform"* for other *fragmentation* to accumulate on. Such *"platforms"* are more accurately referred to as *"implants"* in our *Systemology*. The subject of *implants* will be taken up in more detail later on.

As a transition point into our next area of

focus, *run* the following similarly to the previous process (above):

A. *"Spot a deeply held belief (you have)."*
B. *"What have you done about that?"*

When we handle *imprints* and *implants* in *processing*, we are not "erasing" or "forgetting" things—but we are taking the "weight" off the *significance* and *importance* that has been *compulsively* or *reactively* assigned to things, which is to say, how *much* we are *choosing* to allow ourselves to be the *"effect"* of our own past.

One of the ways to practice with this lightly is to reduce the *"force"* that a *Seeker* associates with *action words* such as "hit," "smash," "break," "explode," *&tc.* As a *process*, you would say the word while visualizing a *mental image* of the *force* (such as the action taking place); then say the word and decide that nothing is associated with it—until the word no longer produces an *automatic reaction* (or *mental image*) of *force*. Note that this does not eliminate the "meaning" of the word.

From experience with *systematic processing*, another way we know of freeing up *considerations* is to knowingly exaggerate "both sides" until the handling of it is under greater *control*. Concerning "*significances*," we might alternate the following PCL on a particular *incident*, *event* or even an *object*:

A. "*Decide that it is important.*"

B. "*Decide that it is not important.*"

It should be understood that our intention here is not to eradicate all *significance* or "meaning" to the things in a *Seeker's* life, or that they enjoy, *&tc*. What we want to do is rehabilitate the full power of personal choice over the *consideration* of *importance*—the kind of "fluid freedom" a "*god-like being*" would ultimately have.

SPIRITUAL IMPLANTING

A full handling of all *spiritual implanting* on the *Backtrack* exceeds what is treated in *Systemology Level-5*. These *implants* typically do not inhibit reaching a basic state of *Beta-Defragmentation*. However, they are sometimes encountered while "*Confronting-the-Past*." Therefore a *Seeker* is introduced to the subject here, so that they are better prepared for when they *do* show up in *processing*—whether now, or when handling more *advanced processing* directly for future progress on the *Pathway*.

In our previous publications—such as the *Systemology Core* volumes—"*implants*" are defined as "platforms" or "patterns" on which *imprint fragmentation* accumulates. This is, however, only part of the story, so to speak. As such, this whole subject may be above the level of *reality* for some *Seeker's* to *confront* on their first pass through the *Professional Course*. It is still a critical area for advancement.

A *Spiritual Being* typically experiences an *"implanting incident"* upon *entry into* a specific *Shared-Games Universe* (*e.g. Beta-Existence*). Other *implanting incidents* show up on the *Backtrack*, particularly in the *"between-lives"* areas (that are intentionally) "hidden" from typical view (*Knowingness*). Such *implants* originate from (or are *created* by) more *"advanced civilizations"* than what is currently present on Earth. *"Implanted Universes"* likely originate from a previous *Universe* (preceding versions of a *Beta-Existence*).

During the long span of our *spiritual existence*, we have maintained various positions of *control*. *Implants* are often efforts to simply *"enslave"* beings. *Implants* have also been used (by *advanced civilizations*) to *"condition"* (or *"enforce"*) a certain *"eth-*

ics" (or else to "*stop*" an individual from *doing* various things). There is evidence on the *Backtrack* to indicate that we have *all* been on *both sides* of this activity at one time or another.

In regards to this present *Universe*, *implanting* is commonly conducted by "hitting" a *Being* with "*electronic waves*" in order to give an "impact effect" to the *commands* or *command-lines*. These are *not* the same type of "*command-lines*" or "PCL" used in basic *Beta-Defragmentation* procedures (*Levels 0 to 4*); but we do *knowingly run* "*implanted commands*" (and *confront* them with high-power *Awareness*) for our advanced *processing-levels*, in order to take some of the influential "impact" or "force" *off* of them.

In order to differentiate between types of *command-lines*: an "*implant-command*" is systematically referred to as an "*implant-item*" or "*command-item*" for *processing* (because it is really neither a *"terminal"* nor a *"concept"* —but we *process* it the same, because it does have *energetic-mass* attached to it).

Most *implanting incidents* are quite distantly "old" on the *Backtrack*, and their remaining *"command force"* (by themselves) is actually quite weak. It is primarily the additional *imprinting* on that *platform* (or *foundation*) that makes their *impact* or *fragmentation* seem more "vivid" when *restimulated* in daily activities—or if encountered unexpectedly when *incident-running* at earlier *processing-levels*.

Generally speaking, only *"advanced"* Seekers will go directly "looking for" *implants* to *run* (as part of *Alpha-Defragmentation*). Material regarding *"implants"* is classified *"advanced"* (by the *Systemology Society*) because the contents of *implant-incidents* and their *"command-items"* should not be "casually scanned" without actually *systematically processing* (*spotting* and *confronting*) what was being *implanted*. Otherwise, we again find un-necessary *restimulation* on the *Pathway* (which can inhibit progress).

Implants and *implant-incidents* can strongly affect clear *"past-life recall."* By its very nature, *all fragmentation* "distorts" our view—but we differentiate between *"implants"* and *"imprints"* for good sys-tematic reasons. For one: *implants* are es-sentially *"artificial imprints"* that originated intentionally from an external/outside (*"other-determined"*) *source*; they are not an inherent part of everyday life. Everyday life is how *imprints* get layered on top of (or superimposed over) a preex-isting *implant*. This is why/how *"im-print-chains"* are manifested and carried from one experience (or *incident*) to the next; and one *"lifetime"* (or even *Universe*) to the next.

Another distinguishing characteristic of more significant (or *"heavy"*) *implant-ing-incidents*, is the amount of *confusion*

59

and *surrealism* experienced—which far exceeds what an individual would find in "ordinary" circumstances (even at relatively "higher" levels of *existence*). Geometric *shapes*, complex *patterns*, false *imprints* (*events/incidents*), and misleading *time/dates*, are all common components (or *facets*) used to give the "*command-items*" a longer lasting impact; because they would otherwise not persist as long as they do.

When a *Self-Actualized* individual maintains high-power *Awareness*, the residual effects of most *basic implanting* can be reduced to the level or degree of an annoying "commercial" or advertisement (relatively speaking). This is what prevents additional *fragmentation* from "stacking up" *again*. But, of course, in lower-*Awareness* states, these "*implanted suggestions*" (from an outside *source*) more greatly affect our "*postulates*" and *considerations* about "*what-IS*" (as treated earlier in this lesson prior to this section on *implants*).

DEFRAGMENTING "IMPLANTS"

There is a basic technique for *"defragmenting implants"* available to *Seekers* that have successfully reached this point of the *Professional Course* (and development on the *Pathway*). We will give more explanation of these "steps" as we go along —and there are other ways to advance this work further (using a *biofeedback device*)—but for present purposes, the basic method of handling *implants* (in *Level-5*) is:

A. *"Spot (or Imagine) an implant-item (in the listed sequence)."*

B. *"Confront it until it ceases to have an effect."*

And based on what we have learned (and

used) throughout this course, the easiest way for a *Seeker* to accomplish this as a *systematic process* is to alternately:

A. *"Spot the command-item."*

B. *"Spot something in the room."*

This basic technique is really not an exercise in *"desensitizing"* or reducing impact of "words." It is important to note that *"command-items"* are/were *not implanted* in "English" (or any language of *Human* speech). Therefore, the best we can do for *processing* is to "approximate" their meaning (and *get a sense* for their original intention) when each *"command-item"* is *"Spotted"* (or knowingly *"Imagined"*).

However, let's do some practice with a seemingly unrelated *non-restimulative* exercise. For this, as you sit in a room (or *in-session*): *get a sense* (or *Imagine*) that each of the surrounding *walls* (in rotation) is telling you something. The statement said is: *"This means ---"* (and then you fill-in various "words" to complete it).

Don't worry about what the "*this*" is; just practice with both standard (phrases used in everyday life) and ridiculous (fantastical) statements—but preferably not using the same one more than once in a row. This will give a *Seeker* an idea of the general "tone" or "style" of the *command-items* one might find in a pre-prepared "*implant sequence-list*" (used for *running* a specific *process*).

Let's do another practice concerning "*Spotting*," "*Imagining*," and "*Confronting*"—this time using a *process* that might have a little more "bite" to it. There is no reason to target anything particularly *turbulent* for its practice—but, of course, as a *real process*, a *Seeker* should *run* whatever "comes up." By this point on the course, what we actually mean by "*spotting*" and "*confronting terminals*" should be well understood.

This is best practiced with eyes closed. You can either use *mental imagery* from *past memory*, *imagine/create* them as new, or even apply *ZU-Vision* (if such skills are available) to *actually see* whatever it is. This does not specifically target *implants* and is for practice only—but it can increase *Awareness* and contribute to *defragmentation* efforts, because it is actual *processing*.

Practice—Terminal: "People"

A1. *"Spot (Imagine) someone that you liked."*

A2. *"Look at them (and confront the imagery)."*

B1. *"Spot (Imagine) someone that you disliked."*

B2. *"Look at them (and confront the imagery)."*

Practice—Terminal: "Places"

A1. *"Spot (Imagine) a place that you liked."*

A2. *"Look at it (and confront the imagery)."*

B1. *"Spot (Imagine) a place that you disliked."*

B2. *"Look at it (and confront the imagery)."*

Practice—Terminal: "Objects"

A1. *"Spot (Imagine) an object that you liked."*

A2. *"Look at it (and confront the imagery)."*

B1. *"Spot (Imagine) an object that you disliked."*

B2. *"Look at it (and confront the imagery)."*

Practice—Motions: "Actions"

A1. *"Spot (Imagine) an activity that you liked."*

A2. *"Look at it (and confront the imagery)."*

B1. *"Spot (Imagine) an activity that you disliked."*

B2. *"Look at it (and confront the imagery)."*

Practice—Motions: "Events"

A1. *"Spot (Imagine) a time that you liked."*

A2. *"Look at it (and confront the imagery)."*

B1. "*Spot (Imagine) a time that you disliked.*"

B2. "*Look at it (and confront the imagery).*"

When *implant-running*, a *Seeker* might sense that a certain *command-item* is actually "located" (as an *energy-mass*) somewhere near them, or perceives it being in a certain "direction." This may not occur; but if it does, a *Seeker* would "*mentally reach*" toward that location in order to "*Spot the Item.*" Otherwise, the ideal intention is to *reach back* on one's own "*Spiritual Timeline*" and *Spot* "when" the "*item*" was *implanted*.

For *implant-defragmentation* to be at all effective, a *Seeker* must really "contact" or "connect with" an *implant item* in *processing*. There may be a sensation of "pressure" or a sense that you have contacted some *mass* or *energy*, similar to when you sense a *reaction* associated with some other kind of "*terminal*" or "*incident.*"

66

The *"charge"* on (or attached to) a particular *"Item"* may not be very strong. Regardless, a *Seeker* repeatedly *"Spots"* it until there is literally *"nothing"* associated with it—*no* sensations of "heaviness" and certainly *no* feeling or desire to actually "obey" (or *"postulate"*) the *command-item* as one's own *consideration* or *creation*.

The same *Implant-Patterns* were used multiple times on the *Backtrack*. Similar to when *Confronting-the-Past* (or other methods of *incident-running*): once a *Seeker* has *"Spotted the Item"* multiple times, if there is no feeling of "relief"—and instead it seems to be getting "heavier" or more "turbulent"—it is likely that the same *command-item* was implanted during an earlier time (*implanting-incident*). Handling the *earliest/first* time is the only way to fully *defragment* any *implants* (or *imprints*) using *systematic processing*.

If there does not seem to be an earlier *implanting-incident*—and yet the *Item* seems to be getting more *"charged up"* —it is quite possible that some *charge/fragmentation* was left on one of the *earlier Items* in the same *sequence-list* (or *platform*) that you are presently *running*. This is easily remedied by looking back at the last few *Items* on your *list* to see if there is any *charge* still remaining there; and if so, just *run* that *Item* some more.

Implant-Running can sometimes require a lengthy *processing session* to complete. The intention is to take any *charge* or *fragmentation* off of an entire *sequence-list* (of *command-items*) that pertains to a particular *Implant-Platform*. In addition to a sense of *"relief"* (even if only minor), there should be no fatigue (or tiredness), sense of *mass* (or pressure), no *reactivity* (or significance), and especially no urge to "comply" with any of the *Items*. At that point, a *Seeker* can "casually" read over a *sequence-list* without concern.

Implanted command-items from a long time

ago do not really have a lot of *influential* power once a *Seeker* is *Aware* of them. But they are what underlies all other *unknowing fragmentation effects* that accumulate (or stack up) as a *Being* continues their experience of existence onward from the *implanting-incident*.

For present purposes, we are mostly only concerned with handling those *basic implants* that *enforce* the *Human Condition* onto an individual. Other *Implant-Platforms* that *enforce* the fixed *reality-parameters* of this entire *Beta-Existence* (or *Universe*) in general, are of an even higher order of magnitude and are researched at much higher-levels of progress on the *Pathway*.

"IMPLANT-PLATFORMS"

In actual practice, once an *Implant-Platform* is fully brought into view—and

Known—the residual *fragmentation* is fairly easy to *confront* or "shrug-off" if a *Seeker* has completed their previous *processing-levels*. "Layers" of *fragmented-energy-mass* are peeled off of these same "platforms" or "foundations" during standard *Beta-Defragmentation* procedures (given throughout the *Professional Course*) —and this is the only reason it is even possible for *implant-running* to be effective at these *upper-levels* of development.

Implants, almost by definition, get their "power" from being *hidden*. Even though a *Being* is "conscious" at the start-time of the event, an *implant* is *"installed"* or *"attached"* during an intense overwhelming and confusing *incident* that may actually include periods of *"unconsciousness"* (when an individual is literally "knocked out"). Much earlier on the *Backtrack*, before an *Alpha-Spirit* could be "hit" in this way, *implants* were often connected to *"aesthetically-pleasing"* (*"beautiful"*) *incid-*

ents that were simply "*hypnotic*" to look at.

Many of the *command-items* seem very extreme or "absolute" in their *wording* (*meaning*)—which generates *just* an intense enough impact to have *any* lasting impression at all. Most of the "negative" tone that is attached to an *Implant-Platform* is simply there to deter someone from *looking* at it; giving the sense that it would somehow be dangerous to remember, and therefore an individual avoids *mentally reaching* to that area in order to ever "*inspect*" it.

In many ways, this quality of "*unknowingness*"—and an individual's "*withdrawal from inspecting*" something—is true of *all fragmentation*; however, with an *implant*, the "loud bark" of its *systematic design* intentionally conceals just how "light of a bite" it actually has. Some of the more "extreme" *command-items* were designed to get an individual to "*postul-*

71

ate" that they should forget the *implant* in order to *protect themselves.* But this *consideration* is made as a result of the *implant* and is not truly *Self-Determined*—and in actuality, the "harm" or "influence" of an *implant* will *lessen* the more it is *confronted As-It-Is.*

It cannot be too strongly emphasized that: the *implanted command-items* were never very powerful as a literal *command* or *control* "over" you. They are *creations* from an *external source.* The real *fragmentation* and *entrapment-to-agreements* occurred when *you* decided to make *"postulates"* and *"considerations"* either during the *implanting-incident* or immediately following it. Our own personal *fragmentation* (in an area) also multiplied exponentially whenever we were responsible for *implanting someone else.*

Systemology Society research resulted in pre-prepared *"sequence-lists"* for *running command-items* of specific *Implant-Plat-*

forms. They are generally *run* at more *advanced processing-levels,* because even in *Traditional Piloting,* the *implants* are properly handled as *Solo-Processing.* To do this fully, a *Seeker* would already have had to have reached a basic state of *Beta-Defragmentation,* either from *Co-Piloting* or by making (at least) a second pass through all materials of the *Professional Course.*

Standard practices for *Solo-Processing* require a *Seeker* to isolate their attention on each *listed-item* individually.

To accomplish this, you might place a sheet of paper over the *sequence-list* so that you can move it down to read each line; or cut an appropriately sized "rectangle" hole out of a piece of paper so that only one *command-item* is able to be viewed at a time. Then you simply *run* each *Item* as described in this lesson—and using your skills (and increased *Awareness*) from previous *processing-levels*—until there is *no* discomfort (*turbulence*) or *reactivity* of any kind while *considering* it afterward.

When *"processing-out"* an *Implant-Platform*, if you start to feel "really good," then take a break. This lets you have that "gain/win" before going back to the *list* and getting additional *charge* off it. After you've taken a break, if the *implant* seems resolved—humorous or ridiculous—scan the remaining *command-items* to see if there is any *charge* remaining (and then, of course, *run* what still does). Taking a break is an important part of the *process*, because sometimes there can be so much *"relief"* from a single *Item* that the whole *Implant-Platform* seems like it *defragmented*, when really it hasn't.

Rather than begin introducing entire *Implant-Platforms* at this late point in the lesson, a *Seeker* can practice *defragmenting command-items* with our specially prepared example (below). This *sequence-list* is not a complete *Platform*; however, our research demonstrated that it is often "added" to other *Platforms* as a deterrent to their discovery. Since we seldom attach this part to the actual *sequence-lists* (that are used for *processing*), we can provide it here, separately—and as a training example that provides actual gains.

IMPLANT DISCOVERY DETERRENT COMMAND-ITEMS SEQUENCE-LIST

1A. *"To know about this is to disbelieve it."*

1B. *"To know about this is to forget it."*

1C. *"To know about this is to become insane."*

1D. *"To know about this is to become unconscious."*

1E. *"To know about this is to become less aware."*

1F. *"To know about this is to become sick."*

1G. *"To know about this is to die."*

2A. *"To talk about this is to disbelieve it."*

2B. *"To talk about this is to forget it."*

2C. *"To talk about this is to become insane."*

2D. *"To talk about this is to become unconscious."*

2E. *"To talk about this is to become less aware."*

2F. *"To talk about this is to become sick."*

2G. *"To talk about this is to die."*

3A. *"To remember this is to disbelieve it."*

3B. *"To remember this is to forget it."*

3C. *"To remember this is to become insane."*

3D. *"To remember this is to become unconscious."*

3E. *"To remember this is to become less aware."*

3F. *"To remember this is to become sick."*

3G. *"To remember this is to die."*

4A. *"To think about this is to disbelieve it."*

4B. *"To think about this is to forget it."*

4C. *"To think about this is to become insane."*

4D. *"To think about this is to become unconscious."*

4E. *"To think about this is to become less aware."*

4F. *"To think about this is to become sick."*

4G. *"To think about this is to die."*

After a *Seeker* *"processes-out"* all of the *command-items* of an *Implant-Platform*, the final (and most advanced) *defragmentation* step is to:

1. *"Spot any decisions (postulates and considerations) you made at the time of the implanting-incident."*
2. *"Spot any times you gave this implant to someone else (or wanted others to be implanted with it)."*

A *Seeker* is now prepared to move along further on the *Pathway*.

The Systemology Professional Course
continues in the next lesson booklet:
GAMES AND UNIVERSES

GLOSSARY

actualization : to make actual, not just potential; to bring into full solid Reality; to realize fully in *Awareness* as a "thing."

agreement (reality) : unanimity of opinion of what is "thought" to be known; an accepted arrangement of how things are; things we consider as "real" or as an "is" of "reality"; a consensus of what is real as made by standard-issue (common) participants; what an individual contributes to or accepts as "real"; in *Systemology*, a synonym for "*reality*."

alpha : the first, primary, basic, superior or beginning of some form; in *Systemology*, referring to the state of existence operating on spiritual archetypes and postulates, will and intention "exterior" to the low-level condensation and solidarity of energy and matter as the 'physical universe' (*beta*).

alpha-spirit : a "spiritual" *Life*-form; the "true" *Self* or I-AM; the *individual*; the spiritual (*alpha*) *Self* that is animating the (*beta*) physical body or "*genetic vehicle*" using a continuous *Lifeline* of spiritual ("*ZU*") energy; an individual spiritual (*alpha*) entity possessing no physical mass or measurable waveform (motion) in the Physical Universe as itself, so it animates the (*beta*) physical body or "*genetic vehicle*" as a catalyst to experience *Self*-determined causality in effect within the *Physical Universe*; a singular unit or point of *Spiritual Awareness* that is *Aware* that it is *Aware.*

alpha thought : the highest spiritual *Self-determination* over creation and existence exercised by an Alpha-Spirit; the Alpha range of pure *Creative Ability* based on direct postulates and considerations of *Beingness*; spiritual qualities comparable to "thought" but originating in Alpha-existence, independently superior to a Mind-System.

ascension : actualized *Awareness* elevated to the point of true "spiritual existence" exterior to *beta existence.* An "Ascended Master" is one who has returned to an incarnation on Earth as an inherently *Enlightened One*, demonstrable in their words and actions; they have the ability to *Self-direct* the "Mind" and "Body" as *Self* (as a "Spirit"); and to maintain consciousness as a personal identity continuum with the same *Self-directed* control and communication of Will-Intention that is exercised, actualized and developed deliberately during one's present incarnation.

associative knowledge : significance or meaning of a facet or aspect assigned to (or considered to have) a direct relationship with another facet; to connect or relate ideas or facets of existence with one another; in traditional systems logic, an equivalency of significance or meaning between facets or sets that are grouped together, such as in *(a + b) + c = a + (b + c)*; in Systemology, erroneous associative knowledge is assignment of the same value to all facets or parts considered as related (even when they are not actually so), such as in *a = a, b = a, c = a* and so forth without distinction.

attention : active use of *Awareness* toward a specific aspect or thing; the act of "attending" with the presence of *Self*; a direction of focus or concentration of *Awareness* along a particular channel or conduit or toward a particular terminal node or communication termination point; the Self-directed concentration of personal energy as a combination of observation, thought-waves and consideration; focused application of *Self-Directed Awareness*.

awareness : the highest sense of-and-as *Self* in knowing and being as I-AM (the *Alpha-Spirit*); the extent of beingness directed as a viewpoint (POV) experienced by *Self* as *Knowingness*.

beta (awareness) : all consciousness activity ("*Awareness*") in the "Physical Universe" (KI, in *Zuism*) or else in *beta-existence*; *Awareness* within the range of the *genetic-body*, including material thoughts, emotional responses and physical motors; personal *Awareness* of physical energy and physical matter moving through physical space and experienced as "time"; the *Awareness* held by *Self* that is restricted to an organic *Lifeform* or "*genetic vehicle*" in which it experiences causality in *beta-existence*.

beta (existence) : all manifestation in the "Physical Universe" (KI, in *Zuism*); the conditions of *Awareness* for the *Alpha-spirit* (*Self*) as a physical organic *Lifeform* or "*genetic vehicle*" in which it experiences causality in the *Physical Universe*.

charge : to fill or furnish with a quality; to supply with energy; to lay a command upon; in *Systemology*—to imbue with intention; to overspread with emotion; personal energy stores and significances entwined as fragmentation in mental images, reactive-response encoding and intellectual (and/or) programmed beliefs.

channel : a specific stream, course, current, direction or route; to form or cut a groove or ridge or otherwise guide along a specific course; a direct path; an artificial aqueduct created to connect two water bodies or water or make travel possible.

circuit : a circular path or loop; a closed-path within a system that allows a flow; a pattern or action or wave movement that follows a specific route or potential path only; in *Systemology*, "*communication processing*" pertaining to a specific *flow* of energy or information along a channel; "*feedback loop.*"

communication : successful transmission of information, data, energy (&tc.) along a message line, with a reception of feedback; an energetic flow of intention to cause an effect (or duplication) at a distance; the personal energy moved or acted upon by will or else 'selective directed attention'; the 'messenger action' used to transmit and receive energy across a medium; also relay of energy, a message or signal—or even locating a personal POV (viewpoint) for the Self—along the *ZU-line*.

condense (condensation) : the transition of vapor to liquid; denoting a change in state to a more substantial or solid condition; leading to a more compact or solid form.

confront : to come around in front of; to be in the presence of; to stand in front of, or in the face of; to meet "face-to-face" or "face-up-to"; additionally, in *Systemology*, to fully tolerate or acceptably withstand an encounter with a particular manifestation without an automatic reactive response.

consideration : careful analytical reflection of all aspects; deliberation; determining the significance of a "thing" in relation to similarity or dissimilarity to other "things"; evaluation of facts and importance of certain facts; thorough examination of all aspects related to, or important for, making a decision; the analysis of consequences and estimation of significance when making decisions; also in *Systemology*, the *postulate* or *Alpha-Thought* that defines the state of *beingness* for what something "*is.*"

defragmentation : the *reparation* of wholeness; collecting all dispersed parts to reform an original whole; a process of removing "*fragmentation*" in data or knowledge to provide a clear understanding; applying techniques and processes that promote a *holistic* interconnected *alpha* state, favoring observational *Awareness* of continuity in all spiritual and physical systems; in *Systemology*, a "*Seeker*" achieving actualized "*Self-Honest Awareness*" is said to be in a basic state of *beta-defragmentation*, whereas *Alpha-defragmentation* is the rehabilitation of the *creative ability*, managing the *Spiritual Timeline* and the POV of *Self* as Alpha-Spirit (I-AM).

existence : the *state* or fact of *apparent manifestation*; the resulting combination of the Principles of Manifestation: consciousness, motion and substance; continued *survival*; that which independently exists.

exterior : outside of; on the outside; in *Systemology*, we mean specifically the POV of *Self* that is *'outside of'* the *Human Condition,* free of the physical and mental trappings of the Physical Universe; a metahuman range of consideration; see also *'Zu-Vision'*.

external : a force coming from outside; information received from outside sources; in *Systemology*, the objective *'Physical Universe'* existence, or *beta-existence*, that the Physical Body or *genetic vehicle* is essentially *anchored* to for its considerations of locational space-time as a dimension or POV.

fragmentation : breaking into parts and scattering the pieces; the *fractioning* of wholeness or the *fracture* of a holistic interconnected *alpha* state, favoring observational *Awareness* of perceived connectivity between parts; *discontinuity*; separation of a totality into parts; in *Systemology*, a person outside of *Self-Honesty* is said to be operating from a *fragmented* state.

flow : movement across (or through) a channel (or conduit); a direction of active energetic motion, typically distinguished as either an *in-flow*, *out-flow* or *cross-flow*.

genetic-vehicle : a physical *Life*-form; the physical (*beta*) body that is animated/controlled by the (*Alpha*) *Spirit* using a continuous *Spiritual Lifeline* (ZU); a physical (*beta*) organic receptacle and catalyst for the (*Alpha*) *Self* to operate "causes" and experience "effects" within the *Physical Universe*.

harmful-act : a counter-survival mode of behavior or action (esp. that causes harm to one of more *Spheres of Existence*)—or—an overtly aggressive (hostile and/or destructive) action against an individual or any other *Sphere of Existence*; in *Utilitarian Systemology*—a shortsighted (serves fewest/lowest *Spheres of Existence*) intentional overtly harmful action to resolve a perceived problem; a revision of the rule for standard *Utilitarianism* for Systemology to distinguish actions which provide the least benefit to the least number of *Spheres of Existence*, or else the greatest harm to the greatest number of *Spheres of Existence*; in *moral philosophy*—an action which can be experienced by few and/or which one would not be willing to experience for themselves (*theft, slander, rape, &tc*); an iniquity or iniquitous act.

hold-back : withheld communications (esp. actions) such as "*Hold-Outs*"; intentional (or automatic) withdrawal (as opposed to reach); Self-restraint (which may eventually be enforced or automated); not reaching, acting or expressing, when one should be; an ability that is now restrained (on automatic) due to inability to withhold it on Self-determinism alone.

hold-outs : in photography, the numerous snapshots/pictures withheld from the final display or professional presentation of the event; withheld communications; in Utilitarian Systemology—energetic withdrawal and communication breaks with a "*terminal*" and its *Sphere of Existence* as a result of a "*Harmful-Act*"; unspoken or undiscovered (hidden, covert) actions that an individual withholds communications of, fearing punishment or endangerment of *Self-preservation* (*First Sphere*); the act of hiding (or keeping hidden) the truth of a "*Harmful-Act*"; a refusal to communicate with a *Pilot*; also "*Hold-Back*."

holistic : the examination of interconnected systems as encompassing something greater than the *sum* of their "parts."

Human Condition : a standard default state of Human experience that is generally accepted to be the extent of its potential identity (*beingness*) —currently treated as *Homo Sapiens Sapiens,* but which is scheduled for replacement by *Homo Novus* (the "New Human").

imagination : ability to create *mental imagery* in one's Personal Universe at will and change or alter it as desired; the ability to create, change and dissolve mental images on command or as an act of will; to create a mental image or have associated imagery displayed (or "conjured") in the mind that may or may not be treated as real (or memory recall) and may or may not accurately duplicate objective reality; to employ *creative abilities* of the Spirit that are independent of reality agreements with beta-existence.

imprint : to strongly impress, stamp, mark (or outline) onto a softer 'impressible' substance; to mark with pressure onto a surface; in *Systemology*, used to indicate permanent Reality impressions marked by frequencies, energies or interactions experienced during periods of emotional distress, pain, unconsciousness, loss, enforcement, or something antagonistic to physical (personal) survival, all of which are are stored with other reactive response-mechanisms at lower-levels of *Awareness* as opposed to the active memory database and proactive processing center of the Mind; an experiential "memory-set" that may later resurface—be triggered or stimulated artificially—as Reality, of which similar responses will be engaged automatically; holographic-like imagery "stamped" onto consciousness as composed of energetic *facets* tied to the "snap-shot" of an experience.

imprinting incident : the first or original event

instance communicated and *emotionally en-coded* onto an individual's "*Spiritual Timeline*" (recorded memory from all lifetimes), which formed a permanent impression that is later used to mechanistically treat future contact on that channel; the first or original occurrence of some particular *facet* or mental image related to a certain type of *encoded response*, such as pain and discomfort, losses and victimization, and even the acts that we have taken against others along the *Spiritual Timeline* of our existence that caused them to also be *Imprinted*.

intention : directed application of Will; to intend (have "in Mind") or signify (give "significance" to) for or toward a particular purpose; in *Systemology* (from the *Standard Model*)—the spiritual activity at WILL (5.0) directed by an *Alpha Spirit* (7.0); the application of WILL as "Cause" from a higher order of Alpha Thought and consideration (6.0).

interior : inside of; on the inside; in *Systemology*, we mean specifically the POV of *Self* that is fixed to the *'internal' Human Condition,* including the *Reactive Control Center* (RCC) and Mind-System or *Master Control Center* (MCC); within *beta-existence*.

internal : a force coming from inside; information received from inside sources; in *Systemology*, the objective experience of *beta-existence* associated with the Physical Body or *genetic vehicle* and its POV regarding sensation and perception; from inside the body; in the body.

invalidate : decrease the level or degree or *agreement* as Reality.

mental image : a subjectively experienced "picture" created and imagined into being by the Alpha-Spirit (or at lower levels, one of its automated mechanisms) that includes all perceptible *facets* of totally immersive scene, which may be forms originated by an individual, or a "facsimile-copy" ("snap-shot") of something seen or encountered; a duplication of wave-forms in one's Personal Universe as a "picture" that mirror an "external" Universe experience, such as an *Imprint*.

perception : internalized processing of data received by the *senses*; to become *Aware of* via the senses.

pilot : a professional steersman responsible for healthy functional operation of a ship toward a specific destination; in *Systemology*, an intensive trained individual qualified to specially apply *Systemology Processing* to assist other *Seekers* on the *Pathway*.

point-of-view (POV) : a point to view from; an opinion or attitude as expressed from a specific identity-phase; a specific standpoint or vantage-point; a definitive manner of consideration specific to an individual phase or identity; a place or position affording a specific view or vantage; circumstances and programming of an individual that is conducive to a particular response, consideration or belief-set (paradigm); a position (consideration) or place (location) that provides a specific view or perspective (subjective) on experience (of the objective).

postulate : to put forward as truth; to suggest or assume an existence *to be*; to state or affirm the existence of particular conditions; to provide a basis of reasoning and belief; a basic theory accepted as fact; in *Systemology*, Alpha-Thought —the top-most decisions or considerations made by the Alpha-Spirit regarding the "*is-ness*" (what things "are") about energy-matter and space-time.

presence : a quality of some thing (*energy/matter*) being "present" in space-time; personal orientation of *Self* as an *Awareness* (*POV*) located in present space-time (environment) and communicating with extant energy-matter.

processing command line (PCL) : a directed input; a specific command using highly selective language for *Systemology Processing*; a predetermined directive statement (cause) intended to focus concentrated attention (effect).

processing, systematic : the inner-workings or "through-put" result of systems; in *Systemology*, a method of applied spiritual technology used toward personal Self-Actualization; methods of selective directed attention, communicated language and associative imagery that increases personal control of the human condition.

realization : the clear perception of an understanding; a consideration or understanding on what is "actual"; to make "real" or give "reality" to so as to grant a property of "being-ness" or "being as it is"; the state or instance of coming to an *Awareness*; in *Systemology*, "gnosis" or true knowledge achieved during *systematic processing*; achievement of a new (or higher) cognition, true knowledge or perception of Self; a consideration of reality or assignment of meaning.

responsibility : the *ability* to *respond*; the extent of mobilizing *power* and *understanding* an individual maintains as *Awareness* to enact *change*; the proactive ability to *Self-direct* and make decisions independent of an outside authority.

Seeker : an individual on the *Pathway to Self-Honesty*; a practitioner of *Mardukite Systemology* or *Systemology Processing*, that is working toward *Spiritual Ascension*.

Self-actualization : bringing the full potential of the Human spirit into Reality; expressing full capabilities and creativeness of the *Alpha-Spirit*.

Self-determinism : the freedom to act, clear of external control or influence; the personal control of Will to direct intention.

Self-honesty : the basic or original *alpha* state of *being* and *knowing*; clear and present total *Awareness* of-and-as *Self*, in its most basic and true proactive expression of itself as *Spirit* or *I-AM*—free of artificial attachments, perceptive filters and other emotionally-reactive or mentally-conditioned programming imposed on the human condition by the systematized physical world; the ability to experience existence without judgment.

spiritual timeline : a continuous stream of moment-to-moment *Mental Images* (or a record of experiences) that defines the "past" of a spiritual being (or *Alpha-Spirit*) and which includes impressions (*imprints, &tc.*) from all life-incarnations and significant spiritual events the being has encountered; in Systemology, also "*backtrack*."

Spheres of Existence : a series of *eight* concentric circles, rings or spheres (each larger than the former) that is overlaid onto the Standard Model of Beta-Existence to demonstrate the dynamic systems of existence extending out from the POV of Self (often as a "body") at the *First Sphere*; these are given in the basic eightfold systems as: *Self, Home/Family, Groups, Humanity, Life on Earth, Physical Universe, Spiritual Universe* and *Infinity-Divinity.*

Systemology : a modern tradition of applied religious philosophy and spiritual technology based on *Arcane Tablets* (in combination with "*general systemology*" and "*games theory*") developed in the New Age underground by Joshua Free in 2011 as an advanced futurist extension of the *Mardukite Research Org.*

terminal (node) : a point, end, or mass, on a line; a connection point for closing an electric circuit, such as a post on a battery terminating at each end of its own systematic function; a point of connectivity with other points; in systems, a contact point of interaction; a point of interaction with other points.

turbulence : a quality or state of distortion or disturbance that creates irregularity of a flow or pattern; the quality or state of aberration on a line (such as ragged edges) or the emotional "turbulent feelings" attached to a particular flow or terminal node; a violent, haphazard or disharmonious commotion (such as in the ebb of gusts and lulls of wind action).

validation : a reinforcement of agreements or considerations as being "real."

viewpoint : see "*point-of-view*" *(POV)*.

willingness : the state of conscious Self-determined ability and interest (directed attention) to *Be*, *Do* or *Have*; a Self-determined consideration to reach, face up to (*confront*) or manage some "mass" or energy; the extent to which an individual considers themselves able to participate, act or communicate along some line, to put attention or intention on the line, or to produce (create) an effect.

ZU : the ancient Sumerian cuneiform sign for the archaic verb—"*to know*," "*knowingness*" or "*awareness*"; in *Mardukite Zuism and Systemology*, the active energy/matter of the "Spiritual Universe" (AN) experienced as a *Lifeforce* or *consciousness* that imbues living forms extant in the "Physical Universe" (KI); "*Spiritual Life Energy*"; energy demonstrated by the WILL of an actualized *Alpha-Spirit* in the "Spiritual Universe" (AN), which impinges its *Awareness* into the Physical Universe (KI), animating/controlling *Life* for its experience of *beta-existence* along an individual Alpha-Spirit's personal *Identity-continuum*, called a *ZU-line*.

Zu-Line : a theoretical construct in *Mardukite Zuism and Systemology* demonstrating *Spiritual*

Life Energy (*ZU*) as a personal individual "continuum" of Awareness interacting with all
Spheres of Existence on the Standard Model of
Systemology; a spectrum of potential variations
and interactions of a monistic continuum or singular *Spiritual Life Energy* demonstrated on the
Standard Model; an energetic channel of potential POV and "locations" of Beingness, demonstrated in early Systemology materials as an
individual Alpha-Spirit's personal *Identity- continuum*, potentially connecting *Awareness* of
Self with "*Infinity*" simultaneous with all points
considered in existence; a symbolic demonstra-
tion of the "*Life-line*" on which *Awareness (ZU)*
extends from the direction of the "Spiritual Universe" (AN) in its true original *alpha state*
through an entire possible range of activity resulting in its *beta state* and control of a *genet-
ic-entity* occupying the *Physical Universe (KI).*

Zu-Vision : the true and basic (*Alpha*) Point-of-
View (perspective, POV) maintained by *Self* as
Alpha-Spirit outside boundaries or considerations of the *Human Condition* and *exterior* to
beta-existence reality agreements with the Physical Universe; a POV of Self *as* "a unit of Spiritual Awareness" that exists independent of a
"body" and entrapment in a *Human Condition*;
"spirit vision" in its truest sense.

96

explore the
Fundamentals of Systemology

All *six*
Basic Course
lesson booklets
in one
hardcover
edition!

start your journey on the
The Pathway to Ascension

All *sixteen*
Professional Course
lesson booklets
in two
hardcover
volumes!

THE SYSTEMOL

Seekers and students of the *Basic Course* and *Professional Course* will also be interested in the *Systemology Core Research Series*. These eight volumes are a complete chronological record of the Mardukite New Thought developments from the Systemology Society, published in 2019 through 2023.

The *Systemology Core* begins with the first professional publication released when the *Mardukite Systemology Society* emerged from the underground in 2019, with: *"The Tablets of Destiny Revelation."*

OGY PATHWAY

The Tablets of Destiny Revelation:
*How Long-Lost Anunnaki Wisdom
Can Change the Fate of Humanity*

Crystal Clear: *Handbook for Seekers*

Metahuman Destinations (*2 volumes*)

Imaginomicon:
Approaching Gateways to Higher Universes

Way of the Wizard: *Utilitarian Systemology*

Systemology-180: *Fast-Track to Ascension*

Systemology Backtrack:
Reclaiming Spiritual Power & Past-Life Memory

PUBLISHED BY THE **JOSHUA FREE** IMPRINT REPRESENTING

The Mardukite Academy of Systemology

THE JOSHUA FREE IMPRINT
JFI PUBLICATIONS

MARDUKITE
ZUISM

mardukite.com